The Calculating Cat Returns

The Calculating Cat Returns

Eric Gurney

Text by Nancy Prevo

A Stuart L. Daniels Book

PRENTICE-HALL, INC.

Englewood Cliffs, New Jersey

THE CALCULATING CAT RETURNS
by Eric Gurney

Copyright © 1978 by
Eric Gurney

Published by Prentice-Hall, Inc.
Englewood Cliffs, New Jersey 07632

Printed in the United States of America
Prentice-Hall International, Inc., London
Prentice-Hall of Australia, Pty. Ltd., Sydney
Prentice-Hall of Canada, Ltd., Toronto
Prentice-Hall of India Private Ltd., New Delhi
Prentice-Hall of Japan, Inc., Tokyo
Prentice-Hall of Southeast Asia Pte. Ltd., Singapore
Whitehall Books Limited, Wellington, New Zealand

10 9 8 7 6 5 4 3 2 1
Library of Congress CATalog Number: 78-61782

ISBN: 0-13-110213-3
ISBN: 0-13-110205-2 pbk.

DEDICATED TO

Phyllis and Art

NOTE: In these days of anti-sexist drives, the E.R.A., the woman's movement, and the clamor for women's rights, along with the general desire to de-gender positions, titles, and other specific references, male or female, trying to depersonalize the personal pronoun in discussing people and animals is a roadblock to smooth-flowing prose. Therefore, in this book, cats are referred to as he or she when those pronouns are proper, otherwise, "he" is used to refer to cats in general. Sometimes, you'll find references to "it." That really isn't fair; you wouldn't describe your best friend in such fashion.

CONTENTS

How come cats get all the soft jobs.

1
What Is
a
Calculating Cat?

Cats are calculating. Of that there is no doubt. If you are new to the world of the feline, you may think that the behavior of your pet is capricious and/or ill-conceived. Those persons who have spent much time in the company of the species know that cat actions are usually well planned and quite purposeful. Cats know *exactly* what they want, and what *they* want may not follow the program you have established for them.

For example—since our friends like familiar surroundings and will usually resist rather strongly a move to a new location, you may have to acclimatize him (or her) to your new abode. There are those who believe that putting butter on a cat's feet will assist the adjustment phase. But you may just have created a new interest in the taste of the better spread.

Some cat lovers follow the theory that if one cat is fun, a whole bevy is better yet. This may produce a certain amount of internal friction leading to rather severe marital problems.

Of course the presence of even one of our furry friends is perhaps the best guarantee that the mouse population in your vicinity will be kept to a bare minimum. No need to explain the affinity between these two. Many a calculating cat has wormed itself into a household in definite need of such protection. A little like the Mafia come to stay.

Anyone who has ever shared quarters with one of the members of the subject of this book has to agree with the familiar adage that "you don't own a cat; your cat owns you." Trite as that may now sound, let it be a warning to those who adopt an adorable kitten; you will soon have a very commanding presence in the form of a full grown cat.

You must, however, do everything to resist this situation from developing. Patience and firmness are necessary to establish a state of detente. If you constantly bear in mind the fact that your cat *is* calculating you will soon learn to ignore some of the more ridiculous demands no matter how insistent he or she may be.

Perhaps the pages that are ahead of you will provide some vital pointers in learning to live at peace with your feline companion or companions.

To acclimatize your cat to a new home, place butter on his feet . . .

and . . .

it will feel . . .

that it has always lived there.

Some family members may feel that there are too many cats . . .

but saying "Either those cats go or I go," may be words you'll regret.

Patience and firmness are needed to establish a viable relationship.

Its maddening to think that cats need do little to stay in shape.

Cats are always ready to lend a helping claw.

There is more than one way to flush out the mice.

Constructing a special door your cats can use is a fine idea . . .

but don't forget to lock it at night.

Some people would rather use a whistle to call their cat.

2
Types of
Calculating Cats

There are those persons who when asked about the nature of the cat or cats with whom they share living space will explain simply that their pet(s) is (are) a Siamese or Domestic Short Hair or Persian or whatever. True as that may be, it is really not very informative, even though such designations are acceptable to the vital statistics bureau.

One example of a pampered cat.

A worker at work.

Except for certain specific physical characteristics, no matter what breed, cats are seen in different ways by different people, or for that matter, by other animals. One way to CAT-egorize, the sub-species of *felis familiaris* (familiar cat) is to consider its basic attitude toward life. For want of more accurate terms we designate them as the Pampered Cats, the Working Cats, and sad to relate, the Tramp cats.

The first group, the pampered, have adopted a life style to which most humans aspire. Among the perks that accrue to this group are such luxuries as meal service on demand, the sort of sleeping accommodations usually reserved for royalty and rock stars. Hair care, attention to nails, and other cosmetic matters can only be approximated by that given to stars of stage, screen, and television.

The pampered feline ignores the more menial household tasks that the second group, the workers, are addicted to. Workers are quick to notice any change in normal household routine. If a crumpled-up, discarded telephone bill escapes from the confines of a waste paper basket, the worker will pursue it to an ultimate resting place behind the living room sofa. Indeed, if the paper doesn't fall to the floor of its own accord and if there is no other available work to be done the worker will tip the basket over. A sort of make-work plan.

The worker is, of course, the mouser par excellence. Not to say that even the pampered one won't rouse herself on occasion to pursue this natural enemy. It is a matter of great pride to almost any cat when he, she, or it is able to present you with the results of a hunt just before devouring the quarry.

Cats also are full of love and devotion

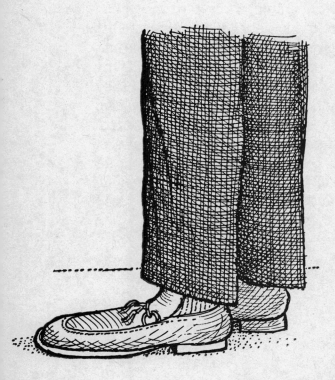

Now for the CAT-egory which for want of a better term has been dubbed the tramp. These are the unfortunates, the outcasts of cat society, denied the comfort of a warm hearth by circumstances of birth or the unthinking cruelty of some of the lesser specimens of homo sapiens. Roaming the streets and countryside, they cadge their meals whenever and wherever they can; from the refuse cans of restaurants, from the kindness of a good samaritan, sometimes from the outer fringes of an affluent household. They tend to be suspicious of strangers and rightly so. They are at the mercy of small boys, snarling dogs, and the town cat-catcher. They lead their lives unprotected by the beneficence of today's welfare state.

And the tramp.

To members of the world at large, both human and animal, the cat appears in different forms. To the bird on the wing he is the world's most dangerous jet-fighter. Yet to the little girl he is so angelic he could only have been made in heaven. The neighbors' dog sees only a menace, more threatening than any movie villain, while the neighbors can only think in terms of a shrilling call. In turn, Grandma has an adjunct to her knitting chores.

So, you see, cats can be all things to all of us. It just depends on your point of view.

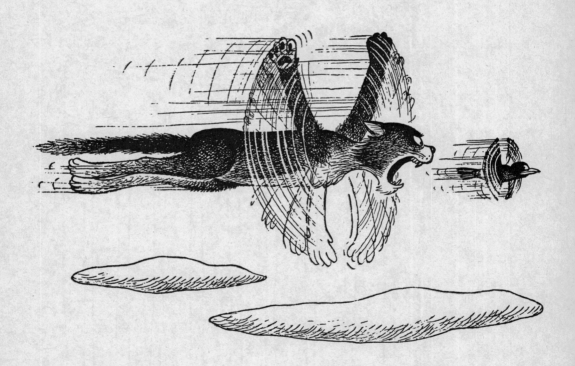

As seen by a bird.

As seen by the little girl.

How the neighbor's dog sees him.

Grandma has a different view.

As heard by nearby neighbors.

Cats will get rid of . . .

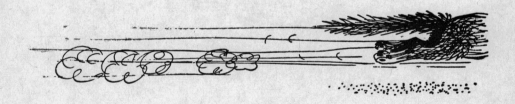

the mice . . .

and possibly your mother-in-law as well.

3 Games Cats Play

Cats love games. At times it's hard to tell if they're playing or using the game ploy as a means of getting even. You may find yourself tripping over one of your friends in particularly suspicious situations.

Cats do, however, like a lot of attention when they are ready to play—that is when *they* are ready. When a cat wants to sleep, he definitely doesn't want to play. A sharp jab with an outstretched paw will tell you so.

Cats usually want to play when you want to do something else, such as read the paper or pay bills. Put your checkbook on your desk, and in no time at all one of your cats will deposit himself directly on top of it. Try to read the paper and he'll find one way or another to discourage you.

A favorite—blocking your effort to pay bills.

If you don't want to play when your cat does, he will come up with some rather astounding ways to gain your attention. Knocking over one of your favorite art treasures is a surefire attention getter.

You never know what a cat will do to get attention.

If your chairs are of the open-back type, either dispose of them completely or never sit in them. They only provide your pet with one more way of saying, "Get up, I want to play."

Never buy a chair with a perforated back. You may regret it.

As pets cats have one great advantage over another favorite species.

Perhaps it isn't big enough.

That's better.

As all cat fanciers know, our friend has one tremendous advantage over that other popular household pet—the use of a litter pan to take care of various natural functions. That's great. Except somehow, no matter how hard you try and to what extreme lengths you may go, your feline pal, usually neatness and cleanliness personified, always manages to spray some litter on the surrounding area.

Careless? Doubtful. More likely some sort of game. He likes to watch you sweep up the litter, feeling that he has provided you with a spare time, fun activity in which he has played a role.

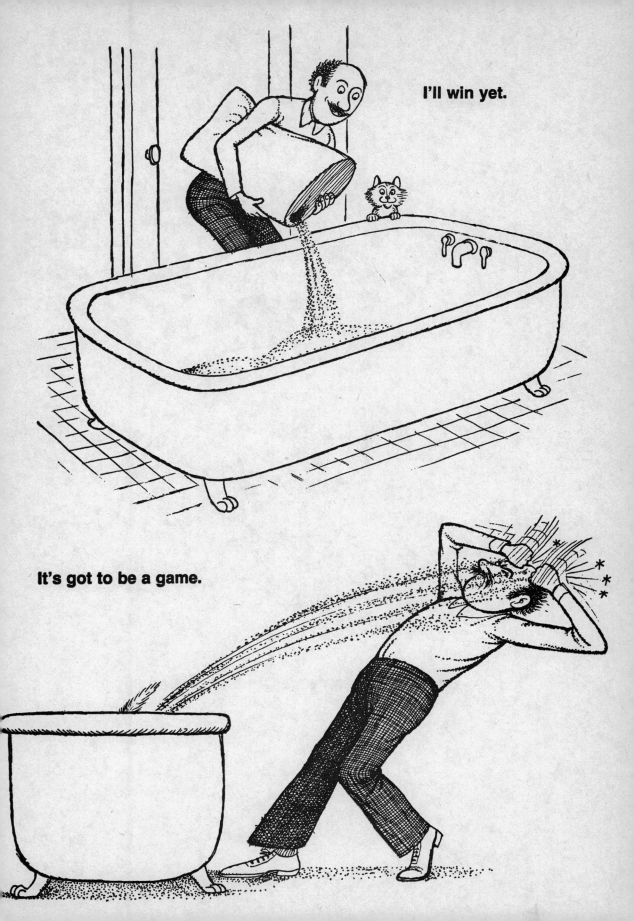

Some cats' greatest delight is in teasing dogs.

Teasing dogs is a favorite gametime activity. Although sometimes otherwise, it is usually the member of the canine species who comes off second best. This often means you'll have to play nurse to an unhappy and injured animal who was only trying to maintain his dignity.

You may never figure out whether your feline friend really wants to play or has just decided to bug you. Another illustration of the inscrutable ways of the calculating cat.

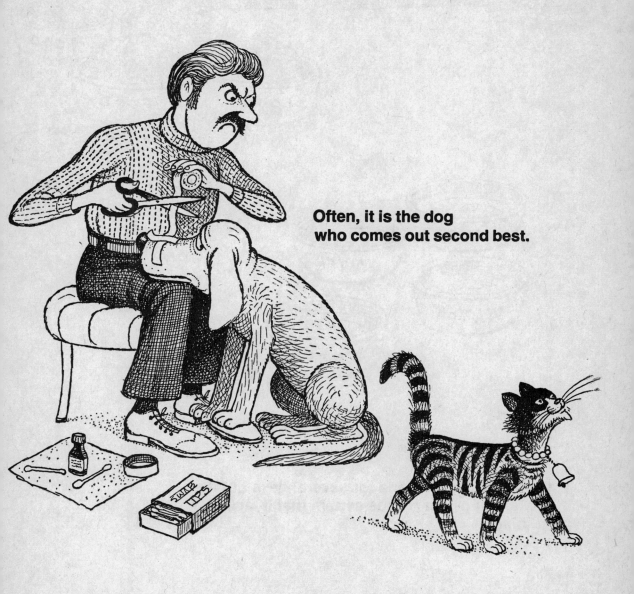

Often, it is the dog who comes out second best.

Cats may be left alone for several days but the loving cat owner makes certain that it lacks for nothing.

4
Some
Gustatory
Experiences

The dining habits of cats are the source of much discussion between cat owners. It is an all too familiar fact that each cat has its own favorite food, and that it eschews almost all other offerings. Among the myriad of brands and kinds of food, canned or boxed especially to please cat palates, there are bound to be some that *may* please your feline companion or companions. Pray that there are—or else life will not be worth living.

Among other characteristics, the feline species may be CATegorized according to eating habits. Among the most prominent, to our distress, is the fastidious eater. Eager to please a member of this group, you may find yourself opening can after can of many different types of packaged foods. Liver, kidney, fish, beef, and all of the many combinations produced by the purveyors of delicacies to the cat world, are offered, only to find the finicky one turning up his nose at all of them. Or, more maddening yet, after you have displayed a dozen or so, is to have him return to the original offering.

Some human parents of cats may go to the trouble of using all of their culinary skills to concoct a special dish to try to satisfy the finicky eater. They may find that this particular one is even more fastidious than the most demanding of restaurant critics.

Then there are the sloppy eaters, those who find it impossible to get through even one meal without stepping in it, or splashing bits on the floor. Then there is the belligerent one who finds it difficult to coexist when it comes to sharing the communal feeding dish.

Just about all cats find houseplants irresistible. They treat them as their own private vegetable patch. Your favorite philodendron or petunia will be short-lived in a cat household. You will just have to alter your interest in indoor horticulture and turn to the cultivation of various types of cacti. Cats show a genuine and intelligent regard for cactus.

Compared to the other popular household pet, cats have a commanding lead in convenience to their owners. They may be left alone for several days at a time, providing their basic needs are met. Of course, the solicitude of some persons is such that the animal is confronted with a bewildering profusion of these basics. Leading to the conclusion on the cat's part that Mommy or Daddy is somewhat loco.

Just after having bought three cases of what you thought were its favorite foods.

The fastidious eater.

A nervous eater.

Selfish.

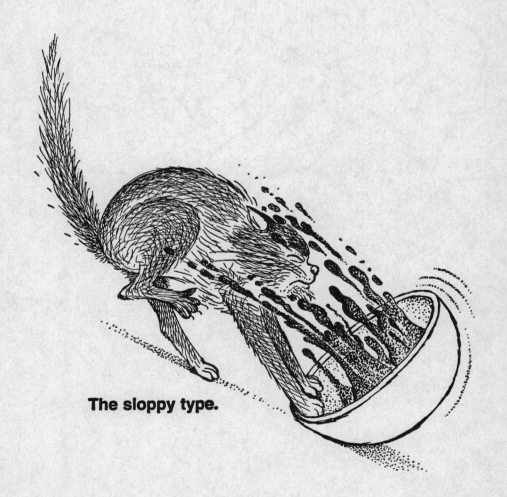

The sloppy type.

Who needs commercials!

The ability to madden even the most loving and dedicated chef.

Most cats love houseplants.

Probably the best deterrent.

Guess who's not coming to dinner.

A bird should make a delicious dinner...

but sometimes things don't work out.

Only rarely does one meet a real glutton.

I'm taking your cat off vitamin pills.

Catnip is supposed to be beneficial for cats. In limited amounts, however. It provides them with lots of fun as they take a trip, but often with disastrous results.

Catnip is supposed to be

very beneficial.

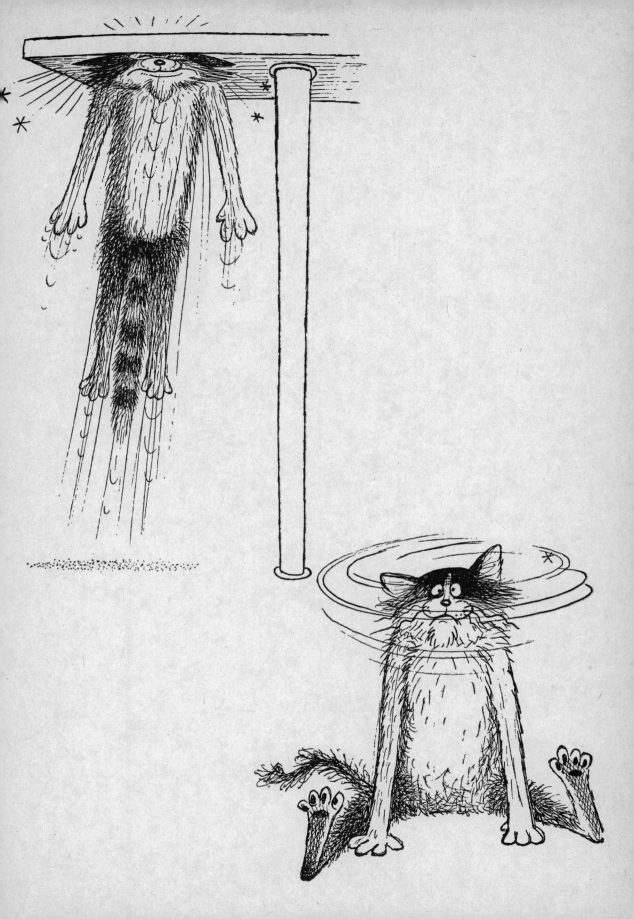

5
To Sleep,
Ah, to Sleep

Cats are able to sleep equally well either in the day or at night. Being nocturnal creatures by instinct, they do find the hour of four o'clock in the morning the ideal time to prowl. If you live in the country and have the habit of putting friend cat out for the night, don't forget to close your bedroom window. That's just about the time he may decide to join you in a playful romp.

Almost any place is considered a proper place for a snooze, day or night.

Forget about buying that special kitty basket that looked so attractive in the pet shop. Cats will choose their own sleeping quarters, often in places that will continue to amaze you.

Cats will always find the most unusual places in which to sleep.

There are those cats who change their resting places every day, while others stick to a familiar location. The warmth that flows from beneath a refrigerator door often provides a favorite spot. Just don't think you'll take anything out of the refrigerator without a struggle.

This is not to say that cats are averse to beds. Especially yours. If you are somewhat indisposed after a rather joyous evening, your friends will be happy to give you some welcome (?) companionship.

If you're indisposed, you'll never lack for company.

"Hey Mom, Albert's on TV," may not mean what you think.

They are particularly happy when you plan to entertain on a wintry day. What is more ideal than a pile of furs and coats for a restful nap?

If you put your friend out for the night .

don't forget to close the window.

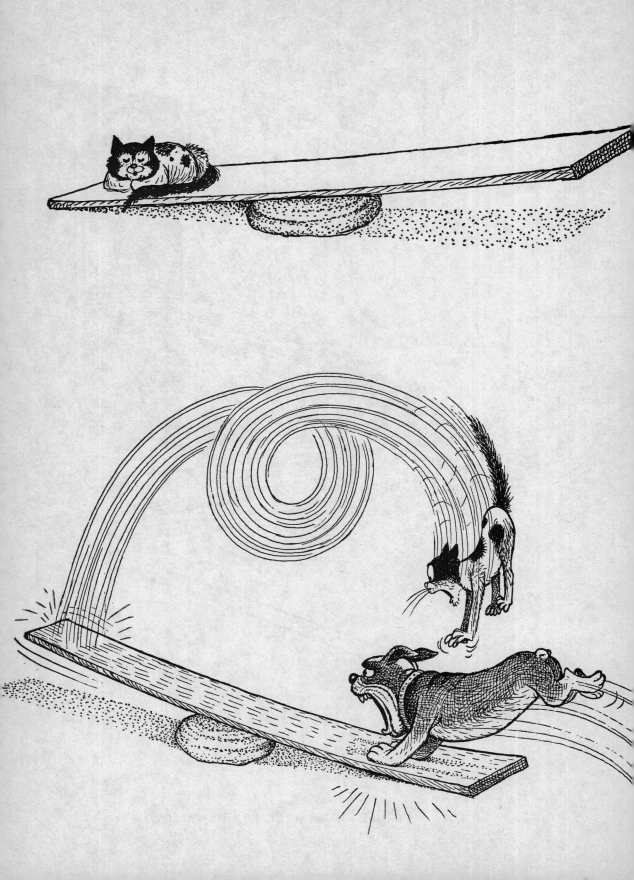

The late, late show.

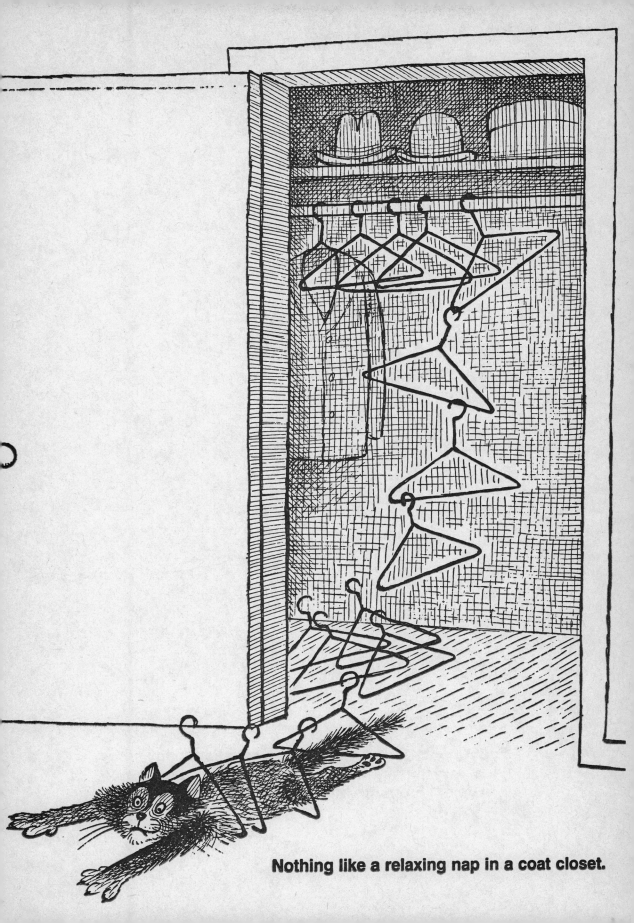

Nothing like a relaxing nap in a coat closet.

"As part of the mating game cats frequently spray a very musky odor. In the cat world this is perfume." From the book, *Raising Your Cat.*

6
Courtship and S-x

Cats love to make love. The net result of this, if you have a female cat, and either aren't aware of the fact or have neglected to have her spayed, is a whole passel of wee ones! These babies then become *your* responsibility. If you don't find any willing takers—you've got problems. So—a word to the wise—Think!

Female cats are capable of producing a litter at about six months of age. If its love call is answered, in a little over two months you may have half a dozen kittens on your hands. Assuming that half of these are female, and this state of affairs continues, inside of two years you could find yourself with several hundred adorable kittens and cats. All other considerations aside, the maintenance of such an assemblage is staggering to even contemplate. Don't neglect the required surgery unless the breeding of cats is your vocation.

Don't let the statement, "Of course it's a male," be your understatement of the year.

There is probably nothing in the world more determined than the male cat's response to the mating call of a female. This call will draw males from miles around and absolutely no force on earth will deter these suitors.

"Of course it's a male" may be the understatement of the year.

When the love call of a female cat . . .

is heard by an amorous male . . .

neither rain . . .

nor hail . . .

nor wind . . .

flood. . . .

fire. . . .

nor gloom of night . . .

will keep him from meeting the object of his indomitable desire.

Cats prefer to be seen at their best

...and are easily embarrassed . . .

He covers it up with a quick wash-up.

7 Travelers

Generally speaking, cats are not too fond of traveling, especially when the trip is originated by someone other than themselves. They prefer to maintain a permanent home base from which to operate.

Oftentimes a cat will make a decision to take a trip entirely on his own. (For a good example see previous chapter.) Other opportunities open up from time to time which cause him to wander. Don't despair. He or she will return. Sometimes with undesirable companions which may create problems.

Many tales have been told about cats traveling hundreds of miles to return to their original residences, having been carted away, either in a planned household move or by some trick of fate. Feel confident that your pet will return sooner or later, unless permanently delayed by a fateful encounter.

If you must travel with your cat, the safest and most reliable method is to use a cat carrying case. Make sure it is securely fastened. Once he is inside the case, you have a certain freedom of movement yourself. The confines of a small boxlike container are not much to a cat's liking, unless it is a box of his own choosing.

An unfettered cat can be a menace inside a moving vehicle since one of its favorite spots is on the dashboard ledge directly in front of the driver. The next favorite location is on your foot which rests on the accelerator.

There are the wanderers, and these more adventuresome types often find unusual modes of transportation.

When three's a crowd.

If you should decide to have your cat accompany you on a trip out of the country, it will need the same immunizing shots that you do. Accomplishing this is not as easy as it sounds but, as in every activity associated with your cat, determination and persistence will pay off.

**Sometimes your wandering pet returns laden
with little strangers.**

A cat carrier is essential. . . .

But it should be escape proof.

No wonder we missed poor old Percy when we moved.

All the comforts of home are provided on certain trips.

LANCE FINANCE Co.

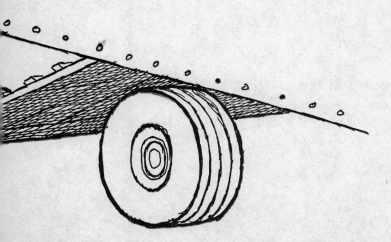

A hefty contribution to the family budget.

8 Friends, Associates, and Other Companions

Certain cats develop their personalities in such a way that they either adopt the characteristics of the humans who are close to them, or they mesh their life styles in some fashion with their owners. Once settled in this pattern, they will find ways to cooperate or help you in your life's work. If you have a difficult assignment they will either help or hinder, depending on their moods.

An artist's best friend.

One noted artist of the abstract expressionist school was able to enlist the cooperation of his cat to capture first prize in an international exhibit.

There are, believe it or not, residential apartment houses whose owners forbid the presence of pets. Smuggling your cat into such a place may present a problem but with the help of your small friend, the problem can be solved.

There are times when your cat will not be as helpful as he might be. While it is far from essential, since cats are highly self-reliant in this regard, some cat owners feel they should give their pet a bath from time to time. You may not think so but once the cat senses this is about to occur, cooperation is the last thought in his mind.

Sometimes your cat is so eager to be close to you that you can hardly sit down without being very careful about your movements.

There are many ways to sneak your cat into a no-pets-allowed apartment.

Carry your favorite oriental rug yourself.

Design a new hat.

Sport a fur collar.

Wear a long evening dress on moving day.

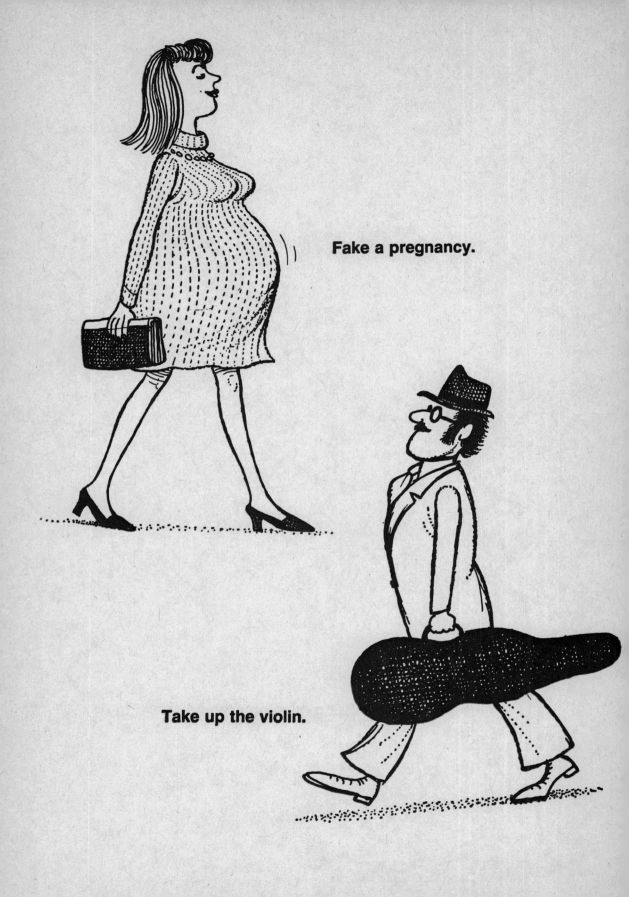

Fake a pregnancy.

Take up the violin.

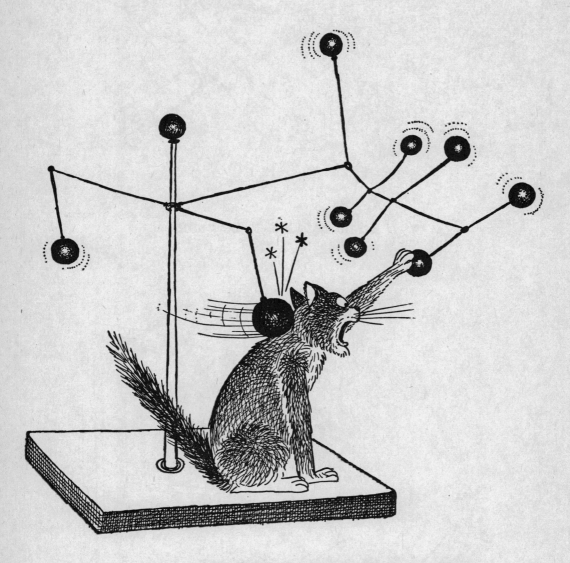

But the sculptor's cat has problems.

Some cats like to be bathed.

Carry him calmly to the bathroom. . . .

and gently place him in the bathtub.

If you are a cat owner, always look before . . .

you sit.

The novice knitter's cat.

The inventor's cat.

A little known fact—Walt Disney's brother Ray would make his rounds on a bicycle accompanied by his cat, Rusty.

Bach, Beethoven and Brahms.

Long live the Calculating Cat.